DEMCO

The Future of Urbanization: Facing the Ecological and Economic Constraints

Lester R. Brown
and Jodi L. Jacobson

Worldwatch Paper 77
May 1987

Financial support for this paper was provided by the United Nations
Fund for Population Activities. Sections of this paper may be repro-
duced in magazines and newspapers with acknowledgment to
Worldwatch Institute.

The views expressed in this paper are those of the authors and do
not necessarily represent those of Worldwatch Institute and its direc-
tors, officers, or staff, or of funding organizations.

Table of Contents

Introduction

A side from the growth of world population itself, urbanization is the dominant demographic trend of the late twentieth century. The number of people living in cities increased from 600 million in 1950 to over 2 billion in 1986. If this growth continues unabated, more than half of humanity will reside in urban areas shortly after the turn of the century.[1]

Historically, world population has been overwhelmingly rural. The number and size of urban settlements increased sporadically over the past several millenia. But the widespread urbanization now evident around the globe is largely a twentieth-century phenomenon: As recently as 1900, fewer than 14 percent of the world's people lived in cities.[2]

Technological change and the availability of vast energy supplies dovetailed in the nineteenth century to foster the development of large, modern cities. In 1800, on the eve of the Industrial Revolution, for example, about one-fourth of the British lived in cities; by 1900, two-thirds of the population was urban. Coal, replacing firewood as the dominant energy source in Europe, fueled this urban growth. It was later supplanted by oil, which has supported the massive urbanization of the late twentieth century, providing fuel for transportation and the consolidation of industrial processes.[3]

Petroleum has also enabled cities to lengthen their supply lines and draw basic resources, such as food and raw materials, from distant points. Cheap oil and economic policies encouraging rapid industrialization together led to a phenomenal surge in urban growth that is still rippling through developing countries.

The authors gratefully acknowledge the comments provided by Peter W.G. Newman, Judith Kunofsky, Larry Orman, Bertrand Renaud, Kenneth Newcombe, Jyoti Singh, and James Chui on early drafts of this paper. Many thanks to Susan Norris for production assistance and an unfailing smile.

6

The evolution of urban settlements, placed in the context of human history, has long been considered a benchmark of social and economic success. But signs of urban stress now apparent around the world call into question the continuing expansion of cities. City dwellers—currently some 43 percent of the world's population—command a disproportionate share of society's fiscal and natural resources and create a disproportionate share of its wastes. Land and water scarcity, inefficient energy use and waste disposal, and the resultant problems of pollution all contribute to the escalating ecological and economic costs of supporting modern cities.[4]

Accelerated urbanization in the Third World has spurred the concentration of political power within cities, leading to policies that favor urban over rural areas. Overvalued exchange rates that reduce the cost of imports, and preferential urban subsidies often make food and other basic goods cheaper in the city, discouraging agricultural investment and attracting people to urban areas. Now, mounting external debts are forcing Third World governments to scale back urban subsidies just as the demand for services multiplies.

The rapid economic growth and abundant resources that contributed to the rise of cities in an earlier era can no longer be taken for granted. Urban areas, larger and more numerous than ever, have outgrown the capacity of natural and social systems to support them. As a result, today's cities may be inhibiting, rather than aiding, efforts to raise living standards in an equitable fashion.

The Growth and Role of Cities

Cities are a relatively recent phenomenon, lagging by several millennia the emergence of agriculture some 12,000 years ago. Agricultural surpluses, expanding populations, and the sense of common interests among peoples of a region fostered the initial growth of urban areas. The first known cities evolved 5,000 years ago on the Nile, Tigris, and Euphrates rivers when traditionally nomadic peoples began to cultivate crops. Food surpluses resulting from successive agricultural advances, such as the harnessing of draft animals and the development of irrigation, enabled farmers to support nascent villages and towns.

"Urban areas, larger and more numerous
than ever, have outgrown the capacity of
natural and social systems to support
them."

Diversification of trade and the production of a wider array of goods
encouraged the continued development of human settlements. Pre-
industrial cities, such as second-century Rome and Chang'an (Xian),
imperial capital of the Chinese T'ang dynasty, arose on nearly every
continent. Advances in science and the arts seem to have depended on
the dynamics of a "human implosion" as the population density of
ancient cities speeded the exchange of ideas and innovations. Urban
historian Lewis Mumford has noted that the maturation of cities in
Greece, for example, culminated in a "collective life more highly en-
ergized, more heightened in its capacity for esthetic expression and
rational evaluation" than ever before.[5]

Despite the importance of cities in past social and economic development, their history only foreshadowed the dominant role cities now
play. Contemporary urban areas are integral centers of production
and communications in a highly interdependent global network. But
particularly in the Third World, where urban growth is most rapid,
the economic gains normally attributed to cities are being offset by
increasingly inefficient use of human and natural resources as a result
of uncontrolled urban expansion.

Urbanization has three demographic components: migration, natural
increase (the excess of births over deaths), and reclassification of
rapidly developing rural areas to cities. Migration is most important
in the early stages of urbanization, as in Africa today, while natural
increase now dominates city growth in parts of Asia and throughout
Latin America. At the current growth rate of 2.5 percent yearly—half
again as fast as world population—the number of people living in
cities throughout the world will double in the next 28 years. Nearly
nine-tenths of this expansion will occur in the Third World, where the
annual urban growth rate is 3.5 percent—more than triple that of the
industrial world.[6]

Latin America, with 65 percent of its people in urban areas, is the site
of some of the world's largest cities: Mexico City and São Paulo
contain 18 million and 14 million people, respectively. By the turn of
the century, over three-fourths of Latin America's 563 million people
are expected to inhabit cities. (See Table 1.)[7]

Table 1: Urban Share of Total Population, 1950 and 1986, with Projections to 2000

Region	1950	1986	2000
		(percent)	
North America	64	74	78
Europe	56	73	79
Soviet Union	39	71	74
East Asia	43	70	79
Latin America	41	65	77
Oceania	61	65	73
China	12	32	40
Africa	15	30	42
South Asia	15	24	35
World	29	43	48

Sources: For 1986 data, Population Reference Bureau, *1986 World Population Data Sheet* (Washington, D.C.: 1986); for 1950 and 2000, Carl Haub, Population Reference Bureau, Washington, D.C., personal communication, August 28, 1986.

In Africa, the least urbanized continent, urban population is growing 5 percent yearly as millions of Africans fleeing environmental degradation and rural poverty migrate to cities. Today 175 million Africans live in cities—30 percent of the continent's total. If current projections materialize, this number will reach 368 million in 2000, a tenfold increase since 1950.[8]

Most East Asian countries—Japan, Taiwan, North and South Korea—have predominantly urban advanced economies. China, now in the early stages of industrialization, is the exception to this pattern. Scarcely 32 percent of its population lives in cities. This divergence is due in part to the strict regulations on internal migration that prevailed prior to 1978, and in part to growing rural prosperity as government policies stimulate agricultural development. Urbanization rates in China have stepped up recently, however, as the government encourages the development of towns and small cities to reduce rural population pressures.[9]

South Asia presents a mixed picture of urban development. Although city dwellers make up a relatively small share of total population in most countries of the region, urbanization seems to be accelerating. India is predominantly rural, with only 24 percent of its 765 million people in cities. Indian cities, however, grow by 600,000 people each month: Large cities such as Bombay, Calcutta, Delhi, and Madras continue to expand, and rural migration to smaller metropolitan areas is rising. The urban share of population in countries such as Indonesia, the Philippines, Thailand, and Vietnam—ranging from 18 to 39 percent—is also increasing rapidly.[10]

Cities of more than 5 million can now be found on every continent. Urban projections for the year 2000 indicate that three out of the five cities with populations of 15 million or more will be in the Third World—Mexico City, São Paulo, and Calcutta. Asia will contain 15 of the world's 35 largest cities. In Africa, only Cairo is now in the 5 million category, but by the end of the century, the continent is projected to have at least eight such centers.[11]

Recent urbanization trends in the Third World are unparalleled historically. Between 1800 and 1910, Greater London's population grew almost sevenfold, from 1.1 million to 7.3 million, an increase now achieved within a generation in many Third World cities. Similarly, Paris took more than a century to expand from 547,000 to about 3 million, a growth matched by some Third World cities just since World War II. Moreover, the population bases to which today's high urban growth rates are adding are often dramatically larger than those in the past.[12]

Most governments in the Third World indirectly encouraged the rise of large cities through a combination of investment and fiscal policies that triggered rapid economic growth in the fifties and sixties. Accelerated industrialization based on capital-intensive industries and imported technologies was promoted to forge links between domestic and international economies. Such policies had a major impact on population distribution, influencing people's employment and residence options. Over the past decade, however, fluctuating energy prices, soft commodity markets, and burdensome external debts have taken their toll on Third World economies. Few countries now have the capital to provide services for or invest in growing urban areas.

As a result of investment and migration patterns, one city, usually the capital, often dominates a country, controlling urban trade with both rural and international markets. The large population in principal Third World cities reinforces their concentrated wealth, power, and status. As the U.N. Fund for Population Activities notes, Manila and Bangkok have more in common with Tokyo and Washington than with their rural hinterlands.[13]

Rapid urbanization is not surprising given that so much national wealth in otherwise poor Third World countries is tied up in one or a few cities. In 1983, an estimated 44 percent of Mexico's gross domestic product, 52 percent of its industrial product, and 54 percent of its services were concentrated within metropolitan Mexico City—home of 22 percent of the country's population. Similarly, more than 60 percent of Philippine manufacturing establishments in 1979 were located in Greater Manila.[14]

The polarization of rural and urban economies in developing countries has two negative side effects. First, the demand for services within the largest cities is so great that few resources are available for investment in other regions. Large cities provide greater economies of scale for certain high technology and export industries. But industrial investments comprise only a small part of an integrated development strategy. Moreover, once metropolitan areas reach a population of 2 or 3 million, they offer no unique advantages to small- and medium-sized enterprises. And the costs of rapidly growing urban areas can quickly outweigh the benefits. *Wall Street Journal* reporter Jonathan Kandell observes that "the cost of supporting Mexico City may be exceeding its contribution in goods and services; the nation's eco-

"Manila and Bangkok have more in
common with Tokyo and Washington than
with their rural hinterlands."

nomic locomotive is becoming a financial drain." Second, because the
success of the principal city becomes so critical to the national economy, the rest of the country is highly vulnerable to economic shocks
or natural disasters that may affect it.[15]

11

Population growth in Third World cities is outpacing city and national
budgets and straining urban institutions. The result is a profusion of
sprawling, unplanned cities in which access to adequate housing,
transportation, water supplies, and education is severely limited.
This pattern of uncontrolled growth reduces urban productivity and
efficiency, affecting not only urban areas but entire national economies.

The sharp income stratifications characteristic of Third World urban
populations result in part from too many people chasing too few jobs.
In metropolitan Manila, 16 percent of the labor force is unemployed
and 43 percent is underemployed. The government's own program
for economic development, including an industrial policy which emphasized capital-intensive rather than labor-intensive industries, has
shut many out of the job market.[16]

Constant increases in urban populations also tax city services to the
limit. In Alexandria, Egypt, a sewage system built earlier this century
for 1 million people now serves 4 million. Lack of investment capital
to upgrade waste treatment and drainage systems has left parts of the
city awash in raw sewage. Most people in large African cities—Lagos,
Nairobi, Kinshasa, Addis Ababa, and Lusaka, among others—lack
piped water and sanitation. A 1979 survey found that 75 percent of
families in Lagos lived in single-room dwellings. Seventy-eight percent of the households shared kitchen facilities with another family,
while only 13 percent had running water. If the urban growth forecast
for Africa is realized, living standards will undoubtedly deteriorate
further.[17]

Low incomes, high land costs, and a dearth of affordable financing
leave a growing number of families unable to buy or rent homes—
even ones subsidized by the government. In Lima and La Paz, the
tin-and-tarpaper shacks of the urban poor are found in the shadow of
tall, modern office buildings. Mexico City has gained notoriety for the

large number of people living in makeshift burrows in a hillside garbage dump. Scenes like these are repeated in shantytowns and illegal settlements ringing cities throughout the Third World.

Growing subsidies combine with weak tax codes to limit the investment capability of national and municipal governments. The Philippine government estimates that at least two-thirds of all new housing being constructed in Manila, where 60 percent of the households live below the poverty line, is "illegal and uncontrolled." In Bombay, at least one-third of the population lives in slums. Although 15,000 dwellings are built there each year by both public and private investors, the government estimates that more than four times that number would have to be built simply to meet current needs.[18]

Excessive urbanization is evident in the increasingly disparate standards of living within cities, and between urban and rural dwellers. World Bank economist Andrew Hamer, reviewing the impact of urban economic concentration on Brazil's development, found that in 1975 São Paulo had less than 10 percent of the country's population but accounted for 44 percent of the electricity consumption, 39 percent of the telephones, and well over half the industrial output and employment. He concluded that "São Paulo has been the beneficiary of preferential public sector treatment for most of the last century [while] large segments of the population and even larger segments of the national territory were subject to 'benign neglect.'"[19]

It is not uncommon for developing countries to allocate only 20 percent of their budgets to the rural sector, even with 70 percent of their populations in rural areas. Yet, in many countries of the Third World, the majority of the population still depends on agriculture for their livelihood and will continue to do so for several decades.[20]

Migrants leave rural areas for a complex array of reasons. High rates of rural population growth and landlessness have foreclosed agrarian futures for many. Some subsistence farmers migrate to cities on a seasonal basis, looking for supplemental employment. But more move permanently in hopes of improving their income propects.

Few Third World governments have adopted national development policies that balance urban and rural priorities. Michael Lipton, an analyst of rural-urban relationships in developing countries, graphically describes the conflicts that arise: "The most important class conflict in the poor countries of the world today is not between labor and [those who control] capital, nor is it between foreign and national interests. It is between the rural classes and the urban classes. The rural sector contains most of the poverty and most of the low-cost sources of potential advance. But the urban sector contains most of the articulateness and power." As a result, the urban classes "have been able to win most of the rounds of the struggle with the countryside; but in doing so they have made the development process needlessly slow and unfair." This strong urban bias in the provision of services, such as education, health, electricity, and water, increases social inequities: It deprives rural individuals of opportunities and societies of sorely needed talent.[21]

13

Urban Energy Needs

Urbanization over the last two centuries has been closely tied to the use of fossil fuels. Coal, used to run the steam engines that powered both factories and rail transport, gave rise to industrial society and the first industrial cities. It dominated the fossil fuel age until a few decades ago, but oil made massive urbanization possible. As world petroleum production turned sharply upward after midcentury, the national and international transportation systems on which cities depend grew by leaps and bounds.

The amount of energy needed to support each urban dweller around the globe is increasing. Both the size and shape of cities are contributing to this trend. In some industrial countries, urbanization has slowed, but others, such as the United States, are still undergoing extensive suburbanization. And in the Third World, where urbanization is proceeding rapidly, energy consumption is on the rise as well.

Whereas rural communities rely primarily on local supplies of food, water, and to a lesser degree, fuel, cities must import these commodities, often over long distances. Likewise, rural areas can absorb their wastes locally at relatively small energy costs, but cities need far more energy to collect garbage and treat sewage.

Urban energy budgets increase as cities expand their boundaries, pushing back the countryside and lengthening supply lines. The amount of energy needed for households, industry, and transportation is closely related to the structure of urban social and economic activity. The efficiency with which energy is used depends less on the size of urban population than on choices regarding land use and transportation. Considerably higher levels of energy are required where settlement patterns are highly dispersed than where people live in close proximity to jobs and markets.

Taken together, the many intimately related yet often uncoordinated decisions made by urban residents and local and national governments shape urban form. Is the city compact or sprawling? Are most of its needs met within a defined region or must resources be imported over long distances? How are wastes handled? The way these questions are answered influences how dependent a city is on external energy resources.

Poor planning leads to inefficient energy use. Suburbs invade the countryside and perpetuate the need for automobiles. Traffic congestion leads to reduced vehicle efficiency and health-threatening pollution levels.

Cities built of concrete, stone, and asphalt absorb and retain solar energy, raising energy consumption in summer by creating the need for air conditioning. A study of 12 U.S. cities showed that while heating was required on 8 percent fewer days in city centers than in outlying areas, air conditioning—a more energy-intensive process— was needed on 12 percent more days, more than offsetting any gains from energy savings on heat.[22]

The amount of energy it takes to satisfy food needs also increases in urban settings. Not only are supply lines longer for cities, frequently extending across national borders, but food shipped long distances needs more processing and packaging. Fresh fruits, vegetables, and livestock products often require refrigerated transport. Of the total energy expended in the food system of the United States, roughly one-third is used in the production of food; one-third in transporting, processing, and distributing it; and one-third in preparing it.[23]

As with food, water needs of large cities often exceed nearby supplies, forcing municipalities to pump and convey water over great distances. Local surface water supplies, frequently polluted by urban wastes, require physical and chemical purification, another energy-consuming process.

Most cities can realize dramatic savings in transport energy use—one of the largest urban energy expenditures—by reducing their reliance on automobiles. Studies of the major petroleum-consuming sectors in the United States, for example, have shown that compared to residential and industrial users, savings in oil consumption in the transport sector have been negligible. (See Table 2.) Fuel-switching and conservation have been important contributors to lowering oil consumption in all but the auto-dominated transport sector.

No single technology has had greater impact on urban form in the last several decades than the internal combustion engine. The first industrial cities, clustered around rail and trolley lines, were limited in size

Table 2: Average Annual Growth of Petroleum Use in the United States by Sector, 1965-85

	Resident/ Commercial	In- dustrial	Electrical Generation	Transpor- tation	Average Growth in Petroleum Use
	(percent)				
1965-73	−3.1	9.9	19.4	4.8	5.1
1973-79	−3.0	2.5	− 6.8	1.8	1.1
1979-85	−4.8	−5.3	−14.0	−0.2	−3.1

Source: *Monthly Energy Review,* U.S. Department of Energy, various issues.

and form by these modes of transportation. But the proliferation of automobiles earlier in this century eclipsed mass transit. Automobiles encourage the growth of suburbs, and give city dwellers an insatiable appetite for fossil fuels. In addition, the urban sprawl characteristic of auto-based societies has forestalled efficiency gains in other areas, such as district heating and some forms of renewable energy that require relatively high levels of population density to be economical.

Automobile-dependent societies like the United States—where individual mobility through private transport is considered an inalienable right—consume far more energy moving people and goods than those relying more heavily on other modes of transportation. When large and growing populations spread out in widening circles, road networks must expand. Commuting distances lengthen and more fuel is required for urban and suburban transportation.

More intensive land use shortens the average distances that urban dwellers travel and strengthens urban transit systems. Public transit becomes more viable when there are more people per stop; as the number of passengers per kilometer rises, the amount of energy used to move each passenger falls.

Australian scientists Peter Newman and Jeffrey Kenworthy have shown that the amount of energy devoted to transport depends on "activity intensity"—a measure of city land use based on the concentration of residents and jobs per hectare in a metropolitan area. In a global sample of 31 cities, including 10 in the United States, 12 in Europe, 5 in Australia, and 3 in Asia, Newman and Kenworthy found that average per capita gasoline consumption in the U.S. cities was nearly twice as high as in the Australian ones, over four times the European ones, and over ten times more than the Asian cities of Tokyo, Singapore, and Hong Kong. (See Table 3.)[24]

In each case, intensive land use correlated with substantial savings in transport energy. The difference between U.S. cities and those in other regions lies in the distances covered and the degree of reliance on automobiles. For example, in Los Angeles, Denver, Detroit, and Houston, the share of population driving to work ranges from 88 percent to 94 percent. In contrast, only 40 percent of urban residents

Table 3: Urban Gasoline Consumption Per Capita, United States and Other Countries

Urban Areas	Consumption Per Capita	Relationship of Consumption in U.S. Cities to Other Cities
	(gallons)	(ratio)
U.S. Cities	416	1.0
Toronto	248	1.7
Australian Cities	218	1.9
European Cities	97	4.3
Asian Cities	40	10.4

Source: Peter W. G. Newman and Jeffrey R. Kenworthy, "Gasoline Consumption and Cities: A Comparison of U.S. Cities with a Global Survey and Some Implications," (draft submitted for publication), Murdoch University, Murdoch, Australia, December 1986.

in Europe drive to work. Thirty-seven percent use public transit and the remainder walk or ride bicycles. Only 15 percent of the population in industrialized Asian cities such as Tokyo commute to work by car.[25]

The distances urban Europeans travel to work and on daily errands are 50 percent shorter on average than similar trips in North American and Australian cities, which have more extensively suburbanized since World War II. Newman and Kenworthy found in these international urban comparisons that land-use patterns are more important for energy consumption than income levels, gasoline prices, or the size of cars.[26]

The link between land-use intensity and gasoline consumption is also evident in a comparison of ten major U.S. cities. (See Table 4.) Residents of Houston and Phoenix—the metropolitan areas with the lowest activity intensities—consume nearly twice as much gasoline per capita as do residents of New York, a metropolitan area with double the number of people and jobs per hectare.

Table 4: Gasoline Consumption Per Capita in Selected U.S. Cities, 1980

City	Gasoline Use Per Capita	Share of Population Commuting to Work by Auto	Activity Intensity[1]
	(gallons)	(percent)	
Houston	546	94	14
Phoenix	512	95	13
Detroit	482	93	20
Denver	462	88	20
Los Angeles	428	88	29
San Francisco	424	78	23
Washington	374	81	21
Boston	374	74	20
Chicago	353	76	26
New York	323	64	31
Average	416	83	22

[1]Activity intensity is a measure of the number of residents plus jobs per hectare in a metropolitan area.

Source: Peter W. G. Newman and Jeffrey R. Kenworthy, "Gasoline Consumption and Cities: A Comparison of U.S. Cities with a Global Survey and Some Implications" (draft submitted for publication), Murdoch University, Murdoch, Australia, December 1986.

Inner-city residents of New York use only one-third the gasoline of residents living in the outer regions of the tri-state metropolitan area of New York, New Jersey, and Connecticut. And Manhattan residents use on average only 88 gallons of gasoline per capita each year, a consumption level close to that in European cities. By contrast, each of the 240,000 suburban residents of Denver's metropolitan area consumes some 1,000 gallons of gasoline per year—more than 11 times that of Manhattan residents.[27]

Once a city becomes dependent on automobiles, inefficient land-use patterns and automobile reliance tend to become self-reinforcing, making the transition to mass transportation more difficult. Unfortunately, Third World cities—where transportation needs are multiplying rapidly—are now repeating the urban development patterns of industrial countries.

19

São Paulo provides a dramatic example of urban sprawl in a developing country. In 1930, São Paulo's population of 1 million covered approximately 150 square kilometers. The city—with a population of 4 million—had spread to 750 square kilometers in 1962, a fivefold increase in area. By 1980, less than two decades later, São Paulo's dimensions had nearly doubled again, reaching 1,400 square kilometers and a population of 12 million.[28]

Poor land-use controls and weak public transit systems have greatly increased auto use at the expense of energy efficiency. But aside from fuel costs, cities reliant on automobiles face substantial hidden costs as well. As a rule of thumb, urban planners must set aside one-quarter to one-third of a city's land to accommodate autos—an extravagant use of an increasingly scarce resource. Road maintenance requires constant infusions of money, while traffic congestion reduces commercial and industrial productivity.[29]

Land-use patterns, population size, and level of development determine both the quantity and nature of urban fuel needs for other purposes, such as domestic and industrial activity. Typically, during the process of development reliance shifts from firewood to fossil fuels. As petroleum output expanded after midcentury, for example, kerosene began to replace wood as a cooking fuel in Third World cities. It was convenient and, for many urban dwellers, cheaper than firewood. The oil price surge of the seventies reversed this trend, catching many countries unprepared for the dramatic growth in urban firewood demand.

Rising fuel prices and a scarcity of foreign exchange to import oil for kerosene have forced residents in hundreds of Third World cities to turn to the surrounding countryside for cooking fuel. As a result, forests are being devastated in ever-widening circles around cities, particularly in the Indian subcontinent and Africa. No forests remain within 70 kilometers of Niamey, Niger, or of Ouagadougou, Burkina Faso.[30]

One country now carefully measuring the loss of tree cover is India, where satellite images have been used to monitor deforestation. One study reports that the areas of closed forest within a 100-kilometer radius of nine of India's principal cities fell sharply between the mid-seventies and early eighties. (See Table 5.) In well under a decade, the loss of forested area ranged from a comparatively modest 15-percent decline around Coimbatore to a staggering 60-percent decline around Delhi.

Unfortunately for low-income urban dwellers, this depletion of fuelwood supplies has boosted prices. Data for 41 Indian cities, including the nine referred to above, show a 42-percent rise in real fuelwood

Table 5: Changes in Closed Forest Cover around Major Cities in India, 1972-75 to 1980-82

City	1972-75	1980-82	Change
	(square kilometers)		(percent)
Bangalore	3,853	2,762	−28
Bombay	5,649	3,672	−35
Calcutta	55	41	−25
Coimbatore	5,525	4,700	−15
Delhi	254	101	−60
Hyderabad	40	26	−35
Jaipur	1,534	786	−49
Madras	918	568	−38
Nagpur	3,116	2,051	−34

Source: B. Bowonder, et al., *Deforestation and Fuelwood Use in Urban Centres* (Hyderabad, India: Centre for Energy, Environment, and Technology, and National Remote Sensing Agency, 1985).

prices from 1977 to 1984. Even though food prices in India have remained remarkably stable, rising firewood prices directly affect the food consumption patterns of the urban poor, who are forced to spend more of their small incomes on cooking fuel. (See Table 6.) Even if India can produce enough food to feed its people by the end of the century, urban residents may lack the fuel to prepare it.

As forests recede from fuelwood-dependent Third World cities, the cost of hauling wood rises. Eventually it becomes more profitable to convert the wood into charcoal, a more concentrated form of energy, before transporting it. This conserves transport fuel, but charcoal typically has less than half of the energy contained in the wood used in its manufacture. Not surprisingly, as urban fuel markets reach farther afield for wood supplies, village residents also suffer from depleted supplies and rising costs.[31]

If firewood harvesting was properly managed and evenly distributed throughout a country's forests, this renewable resource could sustain far larger harvests. But because the demand is often heavily concentrated around cities, nearby forests are decimated while more distant ones are left untouched. As urban firewood demand continues to climb, the inability to manage national forest resources for the maximum sustainable yield could prove to be economically costly

Table 6: India: Index of Real Prices for Food and Fuelwood in 41 Urban Centers, 1960-84

	1960	1977	1980	1984
Food	100	106	102	102
Fuelwood	100	116	140	165

Source: B. Bowonder et al., *Deforestation and Fuelwood Use in Urban Centres* (Hyderabad, India: Centre for Energy, Environment, and Technology, and National Remote Sensing Agency, 1985).

and ecologically disastrous. The future availability of firewood hinges on better management of existing forests and a far greater tree-planting effort than is now in prospect.

Since the oil price hikes of the early seventies, some cities have increased the share of their energy budgets obtained from renewable sources, including wood and agricultural waste, hydroelectricity, garbage-fueled electrical generation, solar collectors, wind turbines, and geothermal energy. As the transition from oil to renewable energy sources gains momentum in the years ahead, it will slow the urbanization process, perhaps even reversing it in some cases.

This effect can be seen in the contrasting prices of kerosene and firewood, the Third World's principal cooking fuels, in rural and urban areas. Kerosene prices are typically cheaper in the city and higher in the countryside because of higher distribution costs in rural areas. Firewood prices, by contrast, are typically lower in rural areas and much higher in the cities. As the shift to firewood and other renewable energy resources proceeds, the economic advantages of living in the countryside will become more obvious.

The cities now relying on renewable energy are as diverse as the sources they are drawing on: Nearly 40 percent of the homes in Perth, Australia rely on wood for heating, and about 26 percent of the city residents use solar energy to heat water. Reykjavik, Iceland, has long used geothermal energy for most of its space heating, while Philippine cities such as Manila derive a growing share of electricity from geothermally powered generating plants. San Francisco is obtaining a growing share of its electricity from nearby geothermal fields and wind farms. In Klamath Falls, Oregon, a city of 42,000 people, more than 500 homes, a hospital, nursing home, and dairy creamery are heated geothermally. A new extension will serve 14 government buildings and several blocks of residences at half the cost of oil heat.[32]

Other cities have increased the efficiency of traditional sources of energy. District heating through cogeneration—an extremely efficient method widely used in the early part of this century—taps the waste heat produced in electric power generation. District heating permits major gains in energy efficiency where urban populations are sufficiently concentrated. Today, European cities lead in the use of waste heat. In an effort to conserve energy and reduce air pollution, Stuttgart, West Germany, pipes heated water from power plants through the city to homes and stores. Tapiola, Finland, has recaptured waste heat since 1953. Enough heat is generated by U.S. power plants to heat all the homes and commercial buildings in urban areas. But this potential resource remains largely untapped in the United States due to urban sprawl.[33]

A few cities, such as Davis, California, have adopted integrated energy planning to reduce waste in all sectors of the urban economy. A survey done in the early seventies indicated that automobiles accounted for roughly half of all energy consumed within the city, while heating and cooling accounted for an additional 25 percent. Now, updated building codes combined with ordinances to encourage solar energy development have reduced the amount of energy needed for internal temperature control. And a low-cost, convenient public transit system has markedly reduced automobile use.[34]

By far the largest share of the world's urban population lives in cities where energy consumption is rising, whether from sheer population growth or poor planning and urban sprawl. Urban planners, by assuming ever greater automobile use, build cities that make it inevitable. In many countries, forms of energy favored by industry or government—including nuclear power and oil exploration—continue to receive subsidies that bias energy development away from renewable sources. But as oil costs rise in the nineties, cities that have encouraged more intensive land use and developed vibrant urban centers and subcenters linked by mass transit will be the most economically successful. Such cities will be able to rely to the greatest degree possible on local, renewable sources of energy to meet their needs.

Feeding Cities

When the shift from hunting and gathering to farming began, world population probably did not exceed 15 million, no more than live in Greater London or Mexico City today. The first cities were fed with

surpluses of wheat and barley produced in the immediately surrounding countryside, since the lack of efficient transportation pre-
vented long-distance movement of food. Residents of early Greek
cities were aware of their dependence on agricultural bounty and
sought to limit city size by design. Lewis Mumford describes the
towns of Greece as "both small and relatively self-contained, largely
dependent on their local countryside for food and building materials."[35]

During the Industrial Revolution this ancient pattern was altered
when Great Britain began to export industrial products in exchange
for food and raw materials. The practice spread, and soon much of
Europe followed this trade pattern. On the eve of World War II, Asia,
Africa, and Latin America, as well as North America, were all net
grain exporters. Rural areas of these regions were producing grain to
exchange for the manufactured products of European cities. Cities in
the industrial countries were tapping not only the food surplus of
their own countryside, but that of industrial lands as well.

These distant sources of food for cities grew in importance after
World War II, as agricultural advances in North America created a
huge exportable surplus of grain. Between 1950 and 1980, the con-
tinent's grain shipments increased from 23 million to 131 million tons.
(See Table 7.) Since midcentury, the growing food surplus of North
America has underwritten much of the world's urban growth. Close
to half of North America's grain exports are consumed in African and
Asian cities half a world away.

Recently, Western Europe—for over two centuries the dominant
food-importing region—has become a net exporter. This shift is attri-
butable to agricultural support prices well above world market levels,
advancing agricultural technology, and near-stationary population
sizes. Like cities in North America, those in Western Europe can now
be supplied entirely with grain produced in the surrounding countryside. In good crop years, such as 1985, Latin America can also feed its
cities.

Although Asia is now the leading grain importer, India and China,
the two countries that dominate the region demographically, have

Table 7: The Changing Pattern of World Grain Trade, 1950-86[1]

Region	1950	1960	1970	1980	1986[2]
	(million metric tons)				
North America	+ 23	+ 39	+ 56	+ 131	+ 102
Latin America	+ 1	0	+ 4	− 10	− 4
Western Europe	− 22	− 25	− 30	− 16	+ 14
E. Eur. and Soviet Union	0	0	0	− 46	− 37
Africa	0	− 2	− 5	− 15	− 22
Asia	− 6	− 17	− 37	− 63	− 73
Australia and New Zealand	+ 3	+ 6	+ 12	+ 20	+ 20

[1]Plus sign indicates net exports; minus sign, net imports.
[2]Preliminary.

Sources: U.N. Food and Agriculture Organization, *Production Yearbook* (Rome: various years); U.S. Department of Agriculture, *Foreign Agriculture Circular,* various issues.

recently achieved food self-sufficiency at least temporarily and are thus providing food for their own cities. Both could conceivably continue to do so if they move to conserve their soil and water resources and encourage more widespread gains in agricultural productivity.[36]

Thus three major geographic regions—Asia, Africa, and Eastern Europe and the Soviet Union—still depend on grain from abroad. Major cities in these areas, such as Leningrad, Moscow, Cairo, Lagos, Dacca, Hong Kong, and Tokyo, depend heavily on grain produced in North America. And the Soviet Union is Argentina's main export market. In Africa, formerly a grain exporter, some of the world's fastest-growing cities are being fed largely with imported grain.

Political instability has increased in regions where the food demands of growing urban populations outstrip domestic agricultural production. In Africa and elsewhere, food-price and wage policies have been key factors in the process of urbanization. Many governments heavily subsidized food staples and other goods either to encourage urban development or to placate politically powerful urban residents. Now, these same governments are caught between the constraints of ballooning budget deficits, soaring foreign debts, and the demands of urban residents accustomed to low-cost goods.

In Zambia, food policies were used in the fifties to encourage growth in the copper-mining industry. Maize prices for European farmers were set at three times the level of those for native farmers, immediately changing income prospects for the two groups. Discouraged from farming by low prices, large numbers of native farmers sought work in mining towns, where consumer food prices were heavily subsidized.[37]

In the seventies, copper prices and government revenues fell dramatically; neither has recovered. Population growth is overwhelming a diminishing job market in urban areas and increasing the number of Zambians dependent on subsidized urban food supplies. A budget crisis forced cuts in the maize subsidy, sparking riots in December 1986. Although Zambian President Kenneth Kaunda restored the subsidies, he noted that they would "divert money that Zambia should spend on development of public services."[38]

Egypt, once a food exporter, now meets 60 percent of its daily food needs with imports bound primarily for urban markets. The government, which has barely recovered from the last spate of bread riots, is politically unable to reduce its $2 billion food subsidy but economically unable to sustain it. This precarious situation is increasingly common: Between 1981 and 1986, more than a dozen food-related riots and demonstrations have occurred in urban areas throughout the world. (See Table 8.)[39]

Food-price policies directly affect rural-urban relationships by providing unrealistically cheap food for city dwellers and discouraging private investments in food production and hence rural employment. Such policies hold down producer prices as well as rural incomes, thereby transferring net income to urban residents. Due to low domestic agricultural prices, the food surplus produced in the countryside may dwindle or disappear. The resulting distortion in the development process helps explain both the increasing reliance on imported food and the attraction cities hold for the rural unemployed.

Table 8: Food-Related Riots and Demonstrations, 1981-86

Country	Date	Triggering Event
Bolivia	July 1983	Drought-induced food shortages
Brazil	Summer 1983	Food shortages in northeast
Dominican Republic	Spring 1984 January 1985	Food price increases Sharply increased prices for basic foodstuffs
Egypt	May 1984	Increased bread prices
Haiti	May, June 1984	Food shortages
Jamaica	January 1985	Food price increases
Morocco	January 1984	Cuts in government food subsidies
Philippines	January 1984	Fifty percent increase in food prices
Sierra Leone	Spring 1981	Scarcity of rice and increased retail food prices
Sudan	March 1985	Food price increases
Tunisia	December 1983	Sharply increased prices for wheat and wheat products
Zambia	December 1986	Cuts in government food subsidies

Sources: U.S. Department of Agriculture, *Outlook and Situation Reports*, Washington, D.C.; various news articles.

Subsidies protect low income urban groups from fluctuating food prices, but for countries with growing populations, they carry prohibitive costs. Several factors limit the potential success of subsidies. To meet standards of equity and efficiency, subsidies must directly benefit a target group. In many countries, however, food subsidies are available to the population at large at high fiscal cost.

To forestall impending food shortages, governments spend scarce foreign exchange that would be better allocated to the purchase of fertilizer or irrigation pumps. Were such investments made, they would expand food output and the national product while creating employment. As the food riots in Zambia and other countries illustrate, the growing disparities between urban expectations and government revenues may lead to increasing social disorder.

Widespread food security has been achieved in those countries, such as China, where urban and rural priorities are in balance. The most effective urban food self-sufficiency efforts are those where city governments orchestrate land use, nutrient recycling, and marketing, as in Shanghai. Increased local production of perishable vegetables facilitates the recycling of nutrients from waste and yields fresh produce at attractive prices, while shorter supply lines reduce dependency on energy-intensive transportation.

As China worked toward national self-sufficiency in cereals, some of its major cities have been seeking self-sufficiency in the production of perishables, particularly fresh vegetables. To reach this goal, Shanghai, a city of 11 million, extended its boundaries into the surrounding countryside, increasing the city area to some 6,000 square kilometers. This shift of nearby land to city management greatly facilitates the recycling of nutrients in human wastes. As of 1986, Shanghai was self-sufficient in vegetables and produced most of its grain and a good part of its pork and poultry. Vegetables consumed in Shanghai and many other Chinese cities typically travel less than 10 kilometers from the fields in which they are produced, often reaching the market within hours of being harvested.[40]

Hong Kong, a city of 5 million occupying an area of just over 1,000 square kilometers, has a highly sophisticated urban agriculture which grows 45 percent of its fresh vegetables. Fifteen percent of its pork needs are satisfied by pigs fed with indigenous food wastes, including some 130,000 tons per year from restaurants and food-processing plants. Relying on imported feed, the city also produces 60 percent of

"Each day thousands of tons of basic plant
nutrients—nitrogen, phosphorus, and
potassium—move from countryside to city
in the flow of food that sustains urban
populations."

its live poultry supply. Some 31 percent of Hong Kong's agricultural land produces vegetables. Fish ponds, occupying 18 percent of the agricultural land, are commonly fertilized with pig and poultry manure and yield 25 to 74 tons of fish per hectare, depending on the particular species and practice used.[41]

In the industrial West, European cities have traditionally emphasized urban community gardens. Following the oil price increases of the seventies, many American cities also launched urban gardening projects, offering undeveloped land to inner-city residents. State governments, particularly in the Northeast, have organized farmers' markets in cities, producing a direct link between local farmers and consumers. Popular with urban dwellers, they are a valuable adjunct to the more traditional roadside stands in heavily populated areas.[42]

Nutrient Recycling

Each day thousands of tons of basic plant nutrients—nitrogen, phosphorus, and potassium—move from countryside to city in the flow of food that sustains urban populations. In turn, human organic wastes—society's most ubiquitous disposable materials—are created. Worldwide, over two-thirds of the nutrients present in human wastes are released to the environment as unreclaimed sewage, often polluting bays, rivers, and lakes. As the energy costs of manufacturing fertilizer rise, the viability of agriculture—and, by extension, cities—may hinge on how successfully urban areas can recycle this immense volume of nutrients. Closing nutrient cycles is thus one of the building blocks of ecologically sustainable cities.[43]

The collection of human wastes (known as night soil) for use as fertilizer is a long-standing tradition in some countries, particularly in Asia. Door-to-door handcarts and special vacuum trucks are used to collect night soil in many of the older neighborhoods of Seoul, South Korea, for recycling to the city's green belt. The World Bank estimates that one-third of China's fertilizer requirements have been provided by night soil, maintaining soil fertility for centuries.[44]

European cities equipped with waterborne sewage systems began fertilizing crops with human wastes in the late 1800s to minimize water pollution and to recycle nutrients. By 1875, nearly 50 sewage farms existed in Britain, some serving major cities such as London and Manchester. These early attempts at nutrient recycling failed for several reasons. The volume of wastes from growing cities soon overwhelmed the capacity of the sewage farms. As cities grew, sites to apply the sewage became ever more distant from the nutrient sources. And untreated human wastes were recognized as a major source of health problems. Strong taboos developed and the practice was halted, resulting in an open-ended nutrient flow.[45]

Recently, attitudes toward nutrient recycling have come full circle. Higher fertilizer prices, a better understanding of natural resource and ecological constraints, and improved waste management technologies have renewed interest in nutrient recycling in industrial and developing countries alike. Such efforts protect scarce urban resources: Municipalities that recycle organic wastes can simultaneously save money, land, and fresh water for other uses. Recycling treated sewage onto farms surrounding cities also enhances urban food self-sufficiency, as indicated earlier. At least six Chinese cities produce within their boundaries more than 85 percent of their vegetable supplies, in part by reclaiming nutrients from human wastes and garbage.[46]

Efforts to devise a comprehensive recycling strategy depend on waste composition, collection, and treatment, and on the disposable wastes that result. Different sewage treatment methods yield different end-products, though they all mimic or enhance natural biological waste degradation. "Wet" or waterborne sewage systems yield raw or treated solids and wastewater effluents for recycling. "Dry" sanitation systems, predominant in developing regions, rely on night soil as the primary recyclable material.

Two waterborne sewage treatment methods are now used. In the first, air, sunlight, and microbial organisms break down wastes, settle solids, and kill pathogens in a series of wastewater ponds or lagoons. Because they are inexpensive and land-intensive, lagoons are used primarily in small urban areas and throughout developing countries. About one-fourth of the municipalities in the United States use wastewater lagoons.[47]

The second type of wastewater treatment uses energy and technology to replicate natural processes. Processing plants receive large volumes of sewage (domestic wastes often mixed with industrial wastes and stormwater), which undergo a variety of physical, biological, and chemical cleansing treatments. This method produces sludge—a substance of mud-like consistency composed mainly of biodegradable organic material—and purified wastewater effluent.

Crop irrigation with wastewater treated in lagoons is practiced worldwide. The effluent is rich in nitrogen, phosphorus, and other nutrients, and represents a valuable water resource, particularly in arid regions. In the Mexican state of Hidalgo, effluents from Mexico City are recycled onto 50,000 hectares of cropland in the world's largest wastewater irrigation scheme. Falling water tables and rising energy costs for groundwater pumping are likely to make this practice even more attractive in the future.[48]

Sewage-fed aquaculture is another way to enhance food production using wastewater ponds. Here, wastewater purification is complemented by cultivating fish on the nutrients and biomass in the lagoons. China, India, Thailand, and Vietnam are leaders in wastewater aquaculture. Fish ponds in Calcutta provide 20 tons of fish per day to city markets.[49]

More than 15,000 sewage treatment plants in the United States handled nearly 98 billion liters of wastewater daily in 1985, generating an annual total of 7 million tons of wastewater sludge (dry weight). The U.S. Environmental Protection Agency (EPA) estimated the nutrient content of this waste at some 10 percent of that supplied to American farmers by chemical fertilizers, worth therefore over $1 billion per year.[50]

Sludge is not usually a complete fertilizer substitute because of variations in nutrient content. Nevertheless, it can provide significant quantities of nitrogen and phosphorus, while offering other agricultural benefits. Sludge is a soil-builder. It adds organic bulk, improves soil aeration and water retention, combats erosion, and, as a result, boosts crop yields. Added to soil or used as incremental fertilizer, sludge can significantly reduce a farmer's commercial fertilizer bill.

Land application of treated sewage sludge has grown markedly over the past two decades. Approximately 42 percent of sludge generated in the United States is applied to land; the rest goes to landfills or incinerators, or is composted. (See Table 9.) Western Europe produces over 6.5 million dry tons of sludge each year, a figure that is expected to rise 5 percent annually as more stringent water pollution controls go into effect. Approximately 40 percent of the sludge produced in Western Europe is now used in agriculture.

Collecting and treating waterborne sewage wastes is one of the largest items in municipal budgets. And sludge processing and disposal accounts for up to 50 percent or more of typical plant operating costs. Recycling can reduce these costs. Wyoming, Michigan, site of that state's largest land application program, discovered that while incinerating sludge cost 13¢ per pound, land application cost only 6¢ per pound. Over 3,000 hectares of local farmland are now fertilized with sludge. In Muskegon, Michigan, where 38 billion liters of wastewater fertilize cropland producing 450,000 bushels of corn each year, corn sales help defray the cost of the treatment facility.[51]

Land application is not only cheaper than most other options, it reduces hidden energy costs that traditional waste disposal methods carry. A great deal of energy is needed to incinerate sludge, a low-carbon material. An EPA survey estimated that 189 liters of fuel are consumed to burn 1 ton of dry sludge; at current annual rates of sludge incineration in the United States (about 1.7 million tons) the energy cost is roughly 322 million liters of fuel. In addition, about 64 million liters of oil is needed each year to manufacture for farm use the equivalent amount of nitrogen lost through incineration alone.[52]

The chemical and biological makeup of sludge must be carefully monitored to protect the food chain from potentially harmful ele-

Table 9: Sludge Production and Disposal in Selected Industrial
Countries, 1983

| | Annual | | Method of Disposal | | | | |
Country	Sludge Production	Farm Land	Land-Fill[1]	Inciner-ation	Ocean Dumping	Unspec-ified[2]	Total
	(thousand tons)			(percent)			
United States	6,200	42	15	27	4	12	100
West Germany	2,200	39	49	8	2	2	100
Italy	1,200	20	55	--------25------		0	100
United Kingdom	1,200	41	26	4	29	0	100
France	840	30	50	20	0	0	100
Netherlands	230	60	27	2	11	0	100
Sweden	210	60	-----------30 -------------			10	100

[1]Includes small amounts for land reclamation and forest application.
[2]Mostly sludge retained in lagoons.

Sources: A. M. Bruce and R. D. Davis, "Britain Uses Half Its Fertilizer As Sludge," *BioCycle*, March 1984; U.S. data from Robert K. Bastian, U.S. Environmental Protection Agency, Washington, D.C., private communication, September 1986.

ments. For example, a high concentration of metals, particularly cadmium, is characteristic of sludges from heavily industrialized cities. In the United States, the EPA regulates wastewater treatment and various aspects of sludge application on land. Some sludges cannot be applied to cropland, but may be used on grazing land. Others may only be used in forests or in ecologically disturbed areas, such as stripmined land.

Composting sludge to produce a humus-like substance that is an excellent soil amendment is also increasingly popular. Although the nutrient value of composted sludge is reduced after processing, other benefits, such as the elimination of pathogens and reduced water content, make this method of recycling more attractive in some situations. More significantly, compost enhances the ability of crops to draw on both natural and synthetic nutrients. Wheat yields in India increased from 28 to 44 percent with each 5 tons of compost added per hectare.[53]

Appropriate technologies and practices for minimizing sewage-related health risks have been widely adopted in industrial countries, but they have not been fully exploited in developing countries. Installing Western-style sanitation is a luxury few Third World cities can afford. Approximately 40 percent of India's 100 million urban households use dry buckets or latrines from which excreta is collected for disposal; only 20 percent are served by waterborne systems and the rest have virtually no sanitation.[54]

The lack of adequate organic waste collection and treatment in many Third World cities results in serious health and environmental problems. Raw night soil provides a microscopic blueprint of the enteric diseases prevalent in a community. Pathogens present in human wastes include hookworm, tapeworm, and the bacteria that cause typhoid and cholera. Unlike treated wastewater, sludge, or compost, the use of inadequately treated night soil in agriculture ensures the spread of these pathogens.[55]

U.S. Department of Agriculture scientists have devised a low-cost composting method capable of killing virtually all pathogens present in night soil. The technique relies on the same principles as those employed in sludge composting but uses less energy, is labor-intensive, and results in a product with a higher nutrient content. Adapting such low-technology solutions to night soil management provides an affordable alternative to financially strapped municipalities.[56]

Although human organic wastes are the single largest source of nutrients from cities, many urban organic materials—household food wastes and the by-products of food processing plants—can be recycled. Composting projects are now taking advantage of everything from brewery and yard wastes to apple pomace, animal manure, paper sludge, and wood chips.

Nutrient recycling is likely to increase in popularity as urban land, water, and energy resources become scarcer and as waste management strategies improve. Recycling sludge through land application and composting wherever waterborne sanitation exists is cheaper and more environmentally sound than any other disposal option. As part

> "Aquifers and wetlands, agricultural and
> open spaces, are all as essential to a city's
> survival as transport networks."

of a broad public health strategy, nutrient recycling can help Third
World cities reach the goals of better health and sanitation, higher
food self-sufficiency, and reduced environmental pollution.

Ecology and Economics of City Size

Cities require concentrations of food, water, and fuel on a scale not
found in nature. Just as nature cannot concentrate the resources
needed to support urban life, neither can it disperse the waste produced in cities. The waste output of even a small city can quickly
overtax the absorptive capacity of local terrestrial and aquatic ecosystems.

The average urban resident in the United States uses approximately
568 liters of water, 1.5 kilograms of food, and 7.1 kilograms of fossil
fuels per day, generating roughly 454 liters of sewage, 1.5 kilograms
of refuse, and .6 kilograms of air pollutants over the same period.
New Yorkers alone annually produce enough garbage to cover all 340
hectares of Central Park to a depth of 4 meters.[57]

Not surprisingly, urban dwellers are far more energy-dependent than
their rural counterparts; suburbanites even more so. Moving large
quantities of food, water, and fuel into large cities and moving garbage and sewage out are both logistically complex and energy-
intensive. The larger and more sprawling the city, the more complex
and costly its support systems become. Nutrient-rich human wastes
that are an asset in a rural setting can become an economic liability in
an urban environment. Indeed, the collection and treatment of sewage is a leading claimant on urban tax revenues, even when it is
processed and sold as fertilizer.

Energy-inefficient buildings and transport, and wasteful refuse disposal practices all combine to raise the fiscal and environmental costs
of urban life. Cities are, in effect, larger than their municipal boundaries might imply: As urban material needs multiply through the
effects of sprawl and mismanagement, they eventually exceed the
capacity of the surrounding countryside, exerting pressure on more
distant ecosystems to supply resources. Aquifers and wetlands, ag-

ricultural and open spaces are all as essential to a city's survival as transport networks, but are rarely ever the subject of urban planners' concerns.

Water, at once the most vital and the most abused urban resource, best illustrates the precarious relationship that now exists between cities and natural systems. The competition between cities and the other major water consumers—agriculture and industry—is rising just as the quantity and quality of available water is declining rapidly.

Many cities are now searching farther and farther afield to augment supplies from overextended or contaminated aquifers. About three-quarters of all U.S. cities rely to some degree on groundwater. Yet only 3 of the 35 largest—San Antonio, Miami, and Memphis—can meet their needs solely from local supplies.[58]

Water-short cities in arid regions are in stiff competition with agricultural interests. Fast-growing Denver suburbs, for example, have purchased water rights on over 19 percent of the 129,000 hectares of irrigated farmland in the Arkansas River Valley. Los Angeles draws water from several hundred miles away. Much of it comes from northern California, pumped over the Tehachapi Mountains some 610 meters above sea level into the Los Angeles basin.[59]

Transporting water can involve enormous energy costs. Mexico City's elevated site means water must be lifted from progressively lower catchments. In 1982, Mexico City began pumping water from Cutzamala, a site 100 kilometers away and 1,000 meters lower than the city. British geographer Ian Douglas reports that "augmentation of the Mexico City supply in the 1990s will be from Tecolutla, which is some 200 kilometers away and 2000 meters lower." Pumping water this far will require some 125 trillion kilojoules of electrical energy annually, the output of six 1,000-megawatt power plants. Construction of these plants would cost at least $6 billion, an amount roughly equal to half the annual interest payments on Mexico's external debt. The city is thus faced with three rising cost curves in water procurement—increasing distance of water transport, increasing height of water lift, and, over the long-term, rising energy prices. Escalating water costs, stringent rationing, or both are likely to prevent Mexico City from reaching the population of 30 million now projected by the United Nations.[60]

In many Third World cities residents receive water that has undergone little or no purification. As Indian economist V. Nath points out, "The cost of providing adequate water . . . to the large cities is extremely high and that of providing safe water can be astronomical." Water containing dangerous levels of toxic wastes, and the viruses, protozoa, and bacteria that cause disease is routinely used for cooking, drinking, and washing. In Jakarta, for example, less than 25 percent of the population's needs can be met by the current supply system. Sewage contamination and saltwater intrusion have rendered many wells useless. In Manila, a city of approximately 9 million people, a scant 11 percent of the population is served by sewers. Road gutters, open ditches, and canals serve as conduits for the raw sewage that regularly contaminates water supplies.[61]

Cities are notorious for their waste and misuse of water. Aging water mains leak profusely. Until recently, few cities were replacing these antiquated pipes. Now, as the cost of obtaining new water supplies skyrockets, conservation is becoming more attractive. London, for example, plans to spend $320 million to replace water mains originally installed during the reign of Queen Victoria some 125 years ago.[62]

Few incentives exist to conserve water or protect it from pollution. Toxic heavy metals and organic chemicals now threaten to taint urban water supplies in much the same way that waterborne diseases did during the Industrial Revolution a century or more ago. Neurological damage and mutagenic birth defects may increase as more and more toxic wastes are assimilated and concentrated in urban environments.

Urban residents are accustomed to paying little for water, while fines levied against industries for dumping toxic wastes in public water supplies are traditionally light or go unenforced. In Peking, a ton of water costs less than a popsicle. Rationing went into effect in mid-1986 but shortages continue to plague the city. One observer calls Peking's water crisis "an inexorably mounting ecological disaster that threatens the well-being of 9.5 million people." [63]

Water supplies are not the only emerging constraint on urban growth. As noted earlier, for many Third World cities the rising price of oil, and hence of kerosene, since 1973 has put pressure on indigenous fuelwood resources. Research on fuelwood prices in India demonstrates a remarkably close relationship between city size and firewood costs. (See Table 10.)

Table 10: India Fuelwood Prices in Major Cities by Size, 1984

Rupees per Metric Ton	Population of City		
	Less than 1 Million	**Between 1 Million and 5 Million**	**More than 5 Million**
Less than 350	Balaghat Darjeeling		
350-400	Srinagar Chikmagalur Asansol		
400-500	Jamshedpur Bhavnagar		
500-700	Bhopal Indore Sambalpur Amritsar Coimbatore Madurai Alleppey	Hyderabad Ahmedabad Bangalore Nagapur Jaipur Madras Kanpur	
Above 700	Gwalior Ajmer Varanasi Howrah		Bombay Calcutta Delhi

Source: B. Bowonder, et al., *Deforestation and Fuelwood Use in Urban Centres* (Hyderabad, India: Centre for Energy, Environment, and Technology, and National Remote Sensing Agency, 1985).

In some smaller cities that are relatively close to forested areas, such as Darjeeling, fuelwood cost less than 350 rupees per ton in 1984. As city size increased, so did firewood prices. In the seven cities with populations between 1 million and 5 million, prices ranged from 500 to 700 rupees per ton. For the three cities with more than 5 million residents, fuelwood cost more than 700 rupees per ton, at least twice as much as in smaller cities. Some small cities also had expensive fuelwood, usually because they were in areas with little remaining forest cover. Thus small cities in India do not necessarily have low fuelwood prices, but all large cities have high prices.

Of all the investments needed to sustain cities, the shortfall is perhaps greatest in the treatment and disposal of human and industrial wastes. The number and concentration of urban pollutants toxic to humans and disruptive of other natural systems rise each year. Unchecked, these wastes pollute the air above cities, enter water and soil, and via many pathways, contribute to poor health. Urban pollutants inevitably transcend city limits; in time, they become the primary contributors to acid rain and the accumulation of carbon dioxide and other greenhouse gases that are changing the earth's chemistry.

Nitrogen and sulfur oxides, ozone, carbon compounds, and suspended particulates such as lead, arsenic, and cadmium foul city air. Reports on the adverse consequences of air pollution in Third World cities with few or no pollution controls are legion. World Bank researcher Vinod Thomas found that automotive traffic is the largest single source of pollution in São Paulo, while industrial processes and power plants were the principal sources of particulates and sulfur dioxide. The more than 8,000 tons of pollutants poured into the air above São Paulo daily have been linked to increased mortality among infants and those over 65 years old. And an estimated 60 percent of Calcutta's residents are believed to suffer from respiratory diseases related to air pollution.[64]

Automobiles—the predominant mode of transportation in many cities today—contribute most heavily to photochemical smog and carbon monoxide pollution. (See Table 11.) Auto particulates represent

Table 11: Sources of Major Air Pollutants in the United States, 1983

	Percentage of Emissions from Each Source by Pollutant[1]					Percentage of all Emissions
	Carbon Monoxide	Sulfur Dioxide	Suspended Particu- lates	Hydro- carbons	Nitrogen Dioxide	
Road vehicles	61	2	16	30	36	41
Electric utilities	—	67	7	—	32	16
Industrial pro- cesses	7	15	33	38	3	13
Solid waste disposal	3	—	6	3	—	2
Miscellaneous	29	15	38	29	28	27
Total[2]	100	99	100	100	99	99

[1]Figures include both metropolitan and nonmetropolitan areas.
[2]Percentages may not add to 100 due to rounding.

Source: U.S. Bureau of Census, *Statistical Abstracts of the United States 1986* (Washington, D.C.: Government Printing Office, 1986).

only a small proportion of total urban pollution; but because they are emitted at street level and are most easily inhaled, auto particulates are among the most insidious, contributing to respiratory ailments, and lead poisoning in children. "Releasing a canister of poison gas on a sidewalk is a criminal act," writes Anne Whiston Spirn of the University of Pennsylvania, "yet those who destroy the emission control devices on their cars, who burn leaded gasoline, who leave their cars running when parked at the curb are engaged in activities no less irresponsible."[65]

In the United States, federal air quality standards and emission control laws have decreased the level of pollutants in most urban areas. But persistent automobile dependence has kept the levels of some pollutants dangerously high. Despite standards set by the Clean Air Act, many cities are still exceeding standards allowed for several pollutants. Ozone levels in New York, Houston, and Chicago registered at least twice the maximum allowable level in mid-1986. In Los Angeles, the level was three times the maximum.[66]

41

Urban pollution problems are multiplying rapidly in many Third World cities where automobile ownership symbolizes economic success. Chinese cities, with their traditional reliance on bicycles and buses for individual mobility, are perhaps the most efficient in their consumption of transport energy. Unfortunately, as Chinese living standards rise, autos are replacing these modes of transport, reducing energy efficiency and raising pollution levels.

While dwindling water and fuel supplies combine with mounting pollution levels to raise the ecological costs of urban life, fiscal costs are rising as well. Laying the foundations of a comprehensive transportation system is essential to an efficient, sustainable city, where goods can compete in world markets. A well-planned transport network raises urban productivity by facilitating the flow of people and goods throughout the city. Higher levels of income equity and social development can be achieved when transportation provides all economic groups with access to jobs and services. Yet developing countries, following the urban settlement patterns of their industrialized counterparts, face severe transport problems.

The demand for transportation in Third World cities is often met with inappropriate remedies that tax city budgets and indirectly encourage more widespread reliance on automobiles. Motivated by the desire to modernize rapidly, most cities in the Third World have invested in politically attractive but extremely costly modes of transportation that serve only a small fraction of their populations.

Expensive underground rail transit systems and elevated roadways have taken precedence over improvements on existing roads and establishment of low-cost bus operations. Costs have risen dramatically as a result: The World Bank notes that municipal governments commonly spend between 15 and 25 percent of their annual budgets on transport-related investments—sometimes much more. Due to high capital and operation costs, high-technology mass transit systems often require continued financial support from government revenues. Each kilometer of a rail subway may cost as much as $100 million, for example. These transportation projects contribute heavily to urban subsidy burdens.[67]

Calcutta's new subway system is a good example of this phenomenon. Between 1972 and 1978, transport investments in Calcutta reached $50 million annually—about 48 percent of the city's total planned investment for all purposes. These costs rose further in the early eighties as the city moved to complete a five-mile-long stretch of subway line between south and central Calcutta. The $650 million spent to date is six times the amount initially projected; more recent estimates suggest that finishing the project will cost nearly ten times the original estimate, or $1 billion. Moreover, government subsidies of at least $1 million each year will be needed to operate the system. Despite the heavy investments and subsidies, the urban poor—the city's single largest demographic group—cannot afford to ride the subway.[68]

A wide gap already exists between the fiscal and ecological costs of supporting urban development in its present context and the resources required to sustain it. Now, industrial and developing countries alike need a new ethic of urban development—one that embraces the concept of the city as an ecosystem in which population size and urban form are matched to available resources. The question policymakers face is how large cities should be in a world that depends primarily on renewable resources. The subsidies that distort the relationship between cities and natural systems and promote waste should be replaced by a set of policies based on more intensive land use in urban centers with a heavy emphasis on mass transit, conservation of resources, and energy efficiency.

A broader analytical framework is needed to guide planners and policymakers in assessing urban investments: namely, a broad social cost-benefit analysis, integrating principles of ecological and economic sustainability, and the principle of financial viability. The benefits of any urban project should outweigh the social costs. And municipal investments should be undertaken only with the understanding that they be financially self-sustaining. Wherever possible, the private sector should be encouraged to provide services, a policy that will heighten efficiency. User taxes can be enforced to reduce waste by maximizing the cost of pollution to individuals and industries.

43

For example, water supplies can be secured and protected through higher prices and land conservation. In New York, where 95 percent of residential units do not have water meters, the average family currently pays less than $100 per year for virtually limitless supplies of high-quality water. Between 1980 and 1985, New York City experienced two prolonged droughts in which demand far exceeded supplies. Nevertheless, the city recently shelved a $6.2 billion plan to increase supplies by skimming water from the Hudson River. Instead, in order to balance New York's water equation, city officials have decided to reduce demand by installing residential water meters, charging higher prices, and encouraging conservation.[69]

Establishing green belts within and around urban areas safeguards and increases local water supplies. Land-use controls and the preservation of wetlands and open space can greatly enhance groundwater recharge and help with the management and recycling of wastewater. A green belt strategy aimed at permanent protection of open lands within and between cities can also mitigate pollution problems and increase urban self-sufficiency in agriculture. Trees and soil absorb many airborne wastes; large expanses of open lands enhance urban air flow.

In Stuttgart, West Germany, a combination of green belts and industrial zoning ordinances have greatly reduced the effect of persistent inversions and weak air flows on pollution levels over the past 30 years. In the United States, Oregon has adopted a statewide green belt strategy. Cities there are required to map 20-year growth boundaries marking open space for preservation.[70]

Creating denser, more efficient cities depends on curbing automobile use. This trend is already under way in many cities, most notably in Europe. Some 2,000 years after Julius Caesar banned human-borne litters from downtown Rome to ease congestion, cars and trucks are now prohibited from entering the city center during rush hour. According to one Roman official, "The message to motorists is to use public transportation to get to work." Stockholm, Rotterdam, Bologna, and Vienna have all banned traffic from various parts of the central city; indeed, virtually all European cities have some restrictions on auto use in force. And in Hong Kong and Singapore, as well as in Korean cities, taxes and financial disincentives discourage the use of private vehicles. The Dutch have taken the most dramatic steps in this area; they have built their streets to discourage auto use and encourage walking and biking.[71]

Public transport can markedly reduce both pollutants and urban energy costs. Bus service in Third World cities, often the only means of transportation affordable to the urban poor, routinely falls short of demand. The importance of buses cannot be overestimated: The World Bank estimates that in 1980, 600 million trips per day were made on buses in cities of the Third World, a figure that is expected to double by 2000.[72]

Mass transit need not be a costly undertaking. Encouraging competition among private companies to provide bus service frees up scarce municipal dollars and increases the choices available to commuters. While autos rarely carry more than two people, one bus may carry up to 80 passengers. Yet a bus takes up the space of only two private cars on the road. Simultaneously reducing the number of private vehicles and setting up special bus lanes allows other traffic to move faster, and increases urban efficiency.[73]

That urban areas have outgrown and overstressed their natural support systems is increasingly clear. American poet and agricultural reformer Wendell Berry has noted that "like farmers, city dwellers have agricultural responsibilities; to use no more than necessary; to waste nothing; to return organic residues to the soil." His aphoristic comment applies to the broader relationship between cities and natural systems. Cities are themselves ecosystems requiring internal balance.[74]

Seeking a Rural-Urban Balance

The formation and growth of cities is an integral part of the economic and social development of nations. The development of early cities was closely associated with the emergence of civilization itself. Over the last two centuries, urban growth has enabled countries to capitalize on the economies of scale inherent in industrial processes, such as manufacturing, leading to the improvements in living standards associated with modernization.

45

Official U.N. projections show urbanization continuing for decades into the future. But as world oil production declines, and the costs of supplying the needs of large cities mount, questions arise over what rate of urbanization best serves national needs. Some national governments are now beginning to reassess the policies that are critical to achieving a better distribution of resources between urban and rural areas.

The optimal balance between countryside and city varies, of course, from country to country and within a country over time. For example, the optimum size of cities will be reduced as the age of oil slowly fades and the age of renewable energy begins to unfold. Oil is a concentrated resource, easily transported in the huge quantities that large cities require. In contrast, renewable energy sources, whether firewood, solar collectors, or small-scale hydro, are more geographically diffuse. Both the ecology and economics of these energy sources suggest that the future will favor smaller cities and those who live in rural areas.

As the energy transition proceeds, the ability of highly oil-dependent cities, such as Houston and Los Angeles, to compete in the world market will be seriously disadvantaged by high living costs and hence, high wages. The cities that move vigorously to improve their efficiency of resource use—energy, water, land, and materials—will strengthen their competitive position. Those that ignore these issues will eventually pay with depressed economic activity and unemployment.

The growth in the world's urban population from 600 million in 1950 to 2 billion in 1986 is without precedent. Because urban expansion in the more advanced industrial societies has come to a virtual halt over the last decade or so, urbanization is now concentrated in the Third World. Part of this urban growth is a response to the needs of industrialization, the pull of urban job opportunities. But much of the urban growth now occurring in the Third World is the result of failed economic and population policies, a process driven more by rural poverty than urban prosperity. Such policies have needlessly distorted the development process in many developing countries.

The official exchange rate that governs the terms of trade between a country and the outside world, and the food price policy that governs urban-rural terms of trade are the principal means of favoring cities. All too often, official exchange rates are set to promote the imports and consumer goods bound for urban markets, sometimes bringing the price of imported food for urban consumers below that of food produced domestically. Policies that keep food prices low discourage investment in agriculture, eventually creating national food deficits. Moreover, the effects of these two policies on rural areas are compounded by the lack of investment in human capital; per capita investments in urban social services such as education and health care are often several times as great as those in rural areas.

Mounting external debts, rising unemployment, and proliferating squatter settlements are among the more visible manifestations of urban-biased development strategies. These effects are nowhere more evident that in Africa, where both per capita grain production and income have been falling for many years.

One way of reaching a nation's optimum rural-urban balance would be to let the market play a more prominent role in economic development. A rate of urbanization determined largely by market forces would almost certainly be more sustainable than that influenced heavily by subsidies. Removing urban bias from economic policy—adjusting exchange rates to reduce the attractiveness of imported consumer goods and food, and adopting food price policies to encourage investment in the countryside—would be a healthy first step in this direction.

"Much of the urban growth now occurring
in the Third World is the result of failed
economic and population policies."

Such a policy shift is not an argument for abandoning all government subsidies, such as those for food, but rather for targeting subsidies to aid the neediest people regardless of where they live. Targeted food subsidies are more cost-effective and produce fewer disincentives to domestic agriculture than blanket subsidies. In the early seventies, the Sri Lankan government discovered that for every extra calorie consumed by the malnourished population under its subsidy program, 13 calories were reaching nondeficit groups. Changing to a targeted food stamp program in 1980 reduced outlays on food distribution from 14 to 5 percent of total government expenditures within two years. Tailoring food subsidies to specific populations allows governments to reduce the overall subsidy burden and the attraction to rural migrants of artificially low food prices in the cities.[75]

47

The urban bias evident in the economic policies of so many Third World countries wastes both human talent and natural resources. The second major adjustment required to reduce urban bias is the transfer of investment in social services to the countryside. A more equitable distribution of education and basic health care services throughout the society would help cultivate the most abundant resource that many developing societies have—their people.

Population policies, environmental conditions, and landownership patterns also directly affect urbanization rates. Countries with ineffective or nonexistent family planning programs are invariably faced with rural populations under greater pressures to migrate to cities. Where the rural environment is deteriorating as a result of deforestation, soil erosion, and desertification, cities are likely to be besieged by ecological refugees. And where landownership is concentrated in a few hands, as in Latin America, landlessness also drives rural people into the cities.

Apart from the optimal rural-urban balance, the question of how urban population is distributed among cities also looms large in countries where a primary city dominates economic and political life. Secondary cities can serve the goals of economic development by acting as conduits for more geographically dispersed investment.

Small urban centers not only provide an alternative outlet for migrants, but also offer local access to agricultural processing industries, farm inputs, and markets. These economic benefits are enhanced when accompanied by decentralized public services, such as field offices of national ministries or regional and provincial administrative offices that can increase rural access to needed services and information.

A few countries have adopted national development strategies aimed at balancing urban and rural needs against available resources. South Korea is one such country. A mix of land-use and industrial location policies was put in place in the seventies to reduce the country's reliance on Seoul, the principal city. At the same time, the Korean government initiated the New Village Movement, a program geared to raise rural incomes and discourage migration from rural areas. More than 450 rural industries have since been established, a major factor in narrowing the income gap between rural and urban households.[76]

China offers another example of a country that has managed to regulate the growth of cities, by restricting migration and investing heavily in the countryside. As a result of the government's strong support for agriculture, incomes of many rural Chinese are higher than those of their urban counterparts. Few Third World governments emphasize agriculture as strongly as China's does, however.

Pressures from international lending institutions to eliminate urban biases in Third World economic policies are mounting, largely because these biases are partly responsible for the soaring external debt of many countries. All too much of the urbanization in the Third World over the past generation has been artificial, supported either at the expense of rural populations or through foreign assistance. In either case it is becoming increasingly more difficult to sustain. Whether vast cities with tens of millions of people—Mexico City or Calcutta in the year 2000, for example—can, or indeed should be sustained is questionable, particularly if doing so requires heavy subsidies from the countryside.

Out of the current reexamination of undervalued exchange rates and food price policies by the International Monetary Fund and World Bank may come much more enlightened national economic development strategies—ones that will serve all the people, not merely the urban elite. The adoption of policies to arrest the growth in external debt and the transition to renewable sources of energy seem certain to slow urban growth. It is even conceivable that in some instances urbanization will be reversed.

1. Number of people living in cities in 1950 from Bertrand Renaud, *National Urbanization Policies in Developing Countries*, Staff Working Paper No. 347 (Washington, D.C.: World Bank, 1981); number in 1986 from Population Reference Bureau, *1986 World Population Data Sheet* (Washington, D.C.: 1986).

2. Renaud, *National Urbanization Policies*.

3. Andrew Lees, *Cities Perceived: Urban Society in European and American Thought, 1820-1940* (New York: Columbia University Press, 1985).

4. Rafael M. Salas, *The State of World Population 1986* (New York: United Nations Fund for Population Activities (UNFPA), 1986).

5. For a discussion of the historical evolution of cities throughout the world, see Lewis Mumford, *The City in History* (Orlando, Fla.: Harcourt, Brace, Jovanovich, 1961).

6. Salas, *The State of World Population 1986*. The definition of an urban area differs from country to country and by region. What is considered a city in relatively unurbanized Africa may not be considered a city in Asia. For the purposes of definition, minimum city size may vary from 10,000 to over 20,000 people. Global and regional percentages used throughout this paper are United Nations averages based on individual country censuses.

7. Ricardo Jordan, "Population and the Planning of Large Cities in Latin America," paper presented at the International Conference on Population and the Urban Future sponsored by UNFPA, Barcelona, Spain, May 19-22, 1986; population projection for Latin America in the year 2000 from Population Reference Bureau, *1986 World Population Data Sheet*.

8. Aderanti Adepoju, "Population and the Planning of Large Cities in Africa," paper presented at UNFPA Conference.

9. Aprodicio A. Laquian, "Population and the Planning of Large Cities in Asia," paper presented at UNFPA conference.

10. Ibid.; monthly additions to population of Indian cities from World Bank, *Urban Transport: A World Bank Policy Study* (Washington, D.C.: 1986).

11. Salas, *The State of World Population 1986*.

12. Lees, *Cities Perceived*.

52

13. Salas, *The State of World Population 1986.*

14. Jorge E. Hardoy and David Satterthwaite, "Third World Cities and the Environment of Poverty," *Geoforum*, Vol. 15, No. 3, 1984.

15. For a discussion of economies of scale and city size, see Dennis A. Rondinelli, "Metropolitan Growth and Secondary Cities Development Policy," *Habitat International*, Vol. 10, No. 1/2, 1986; Jonathan Kandell, "Nation in Jeopardy: Mexico City's Growth Once Fostered, Turns into Economic Burden," *Wall Street Journal*, October 4, 1985.

16. United Nations Department of International Economic and Social Affairs (DIESA), *Population Growth and Policies in Mega-Cities: Metro Manila*, Population Policy Paper No. 5 (New York: 1986).

17. Jeffrey Bartholet, "Mediterranean's 'Pearl' Now Awash in Raw Sewage," *Washington Post*, August 21, 1986; survey on African households from Adepoju, "Large Cities in Africa."

18. DIESA, *Population Growth and Policies in Mega-Cities: Metro Manila*; DIESA, *Population Growth and Policies in Mega-Cities: Bombay*, Population Policy Paper No. 6 (New York: 1986).

19. Andrew Hamer, *Brazilian Industrialization and Economic Concentration in São Paulo: A Survey* (Washington, D.C.: World Bank, 1982).

20. Michael P. Todaro and Jerry Stilkind, *City Bias and Rural Neglect: The Dilemma of Urban Development* (New York: Population Council, 1981).

21. Michael Lipton, "Urban Bias and Food Policy in Poor Countries," *Food Policy*, November 1975.

22. Anne Whiston Spirn, *The Granite Garden: Urban Nature and Human Design* (New York: Basic Books, 1984).

23. David Pimentel, *Handbook of Energy Utilization in Agriculture* (Boca Raton, Fla.: CRC Press, 1980).

24. Peter W.G. Newman and Jeffrey R. Kenworthy, "Gasoline Consumption and Cities: A Comparison of U.S. Cities with a Global Survey and Some Implications" (draft submitted for publication), Murdoch University, Murdoch, Western Australia, December 1986; additional information on land use,

transportation, and energy use can be found in Peter W.G. Newman and Trevor S. Hogan, "Urban Density and Transport: A Simple Model Based on Three City Types," Transport Research Papers, Department of Environmental Science, Murdoch University, Murdoch, Western Australia, January 1987; Jeffrey R. Kenworthy, "Transport Energy Conservation through Urban Planning and Lifestyle Changes: Some Fundamental Choices for Perth," background paper for development of a state conservation strategy for Western Australia, no date.

53

25. Newman and Kenworthy, "Gasoline Consumption and Cities."

26. Ibid.

27. Ibid.

28. World Bank, *Urban Transport*.

29. David Morris, *Self-Reliant Cities: Energy and the Transformation of Urban America* (Washington, D.C.: Institute for Local Self-Reliance, 1982).

30. Data on forest loss from Sandra Postel, "Protecting Forests," in Lester R. Brown et al., *State of the World 1984* (New York: W.W. Norton & Co., 1984).

31. The energy efficiency of charcoal-making is roughly twice the yield by weight from the wood burned. Energy efficiency ranges from 20 to 50 percent, depending on the type of charcoal production method used, whether with earthen mounds or steel kilns. See Gerald Foley, *Charcoal Making in Developing Countries* (Washington, D.C.: Earthscan/International Institute for Environment and Development, 1986).

32. Information on district heating in European cities from Spirn, *The Granite Garden*; information on U.S. cities from Herman E. Koenig, "The Scientific and Technological Context of Today's Urban Problems," from "Critical Urban Issues in the 1980s: Problems and Responses," a discussion series sponsored by Urban Affairs Programs, Michigan State University, East Lansing, Mich., May 1984.

33. Data for Perth from Peter W.G. Newman, "Domestic Energy Use in Australian Cities," *Urban Ecology*, No. 7, 1982; data for renewable energy in San Francisco, Reykjavik, and Manila, from Christopher Flavin and Cynthia Pollock, "Harnessing Renewable Energy," in Lester R. Brown et al., *State of the World 1985* (New York: W.W. Norton & Co., 1985); information on Klamath Falls, Ore., from Morris, *Self-Reliant Cities*; Klamath Falls population from Klamath Falls Chamber of Commerce, private communication, April 2, 1987.

34. Spirn, *The Granite Garden*.

35. Mumford, *The City in History*.

36. Food self-sufficiency in India and China derived by Worldwatch from United States Department of Agriculture (USDA), Foreign Agriculture Service (FAS), *Foreign Agriculture Circular—Grain Reference Tables For Individual Countries* (Washington,D.C.: various years); USDA, FAS, *Foreign Agriculture Circular—Rice Reference Tables for Individual Countries* (Washington, D.C.: various years).

37. A detailed discussion of different kinds of subsidies and their various ramifications can be found in Grant Scobie, "Food Consumption Policies," (background paper prepared for World Bank, *World Development Report 1986*), Ruakura Agricultural Research Center, Hamilton, New Zealand, August, 1985.

38. "Food Riots in Zambia; Borders Are Closed," *New York Times*, December 10, 1986; "Zambia Halts Food Increases After Rioting and 11 Deaths," *New York Times*, December 12, 1986.

39. Christopher S. Wren, "Cairo Seems to Lose a Chance to Prosper in a Time of Peace," *New York Times*, August 23, 1986; and John Kifner, "The Egyptian Economy Has No Place To Turn," *New York Times*, July 6, 1986.

40. Yue-Man Yeung, "Urban Agriculture in Asia," The Food Energy Nexus Programme of the United Nations University, Tokyo, September, 1985.

41. Ibid.

42. John Spitler, "Many Hard-Pressed U.S. Farmers Sell Produce Directly to Public," *Christian Science Monitor*, November 12, 1986.

43. Nutrients present in human wastes that are lost through disposal is a Worldwatch Institute estimate based on figures from A.M. Bruce and R.D. Davis, "Britain Uses Half Its Fertilizer As Sludge," *BioCycle*, March 1984; Robert K. Bastian and Jay Benforado, "Waste Treatment: Doing What Comes Naturally," *Technology Review*, February/March 1983; Hillel I. Shuval et al., *Wastewater Irrigation in Developing Countries: Health Effects and Technical Solutions* (Washington, D.C.: United Nations Development Program and World Bank, 1986); U.S. Environmental Protection Agency (EPA), *Environmental Regulations and Technology: Use and Disposal of Municipal Wastewater Sludge* (Washington, D.C.: 1984).

44. Seoul's night soil collection system described in DIESA, *Population Growth and Policies in Mega-Cities: Seoul* (New York: 1986); China's use of night soil in Hillel I. Shuval et al., *Appropriate Technology for Water Supply and Sanitation: Night-soil Composting* (Washington, D.C.: World Bank, 1981).

45. The First Royal Commission in England set a precedent with guidelines and suggestions for the land application of sewage wastes in 1865. A detailed discussion of the history of nutrient recycling in European cities can be found in Shuval et al., *Wastewater Irrigation in Developing Countries*.

46. Yeung, "Urban Agriculture in Asia."

47. EPA, *Primer for Wastewater Treatment* (Washington, D.C.: 1984).

48. Shuval et al., *Wastewater Irrigation in Developing Countries*.

49. An excellent discussion of wastewater aquaculture practice in a number of countries can be found in Peter Edwards, *Aquaculture: A Component of Low Cost Sanitation Technology* (Washington, D.C.: United Nations Development Program and World Bank, 1985).

50. Robert K. Bastian, EPA, Washington, D.C., private communication, September 1986.

51. Judy Licht and Jeff Johnson, "Sludge is an Awful Thing to Waste," *Sierra*, March/April 1986; Dawn Schauer, "Saving Money While Land Applying," *BioCycle*, November/December 1986.

52. John M. Walker, "Using Municipal Sewage Sludge on Land Makes Sense," *Compost Science/Land Utilization*, September/October 1979.

53. S.C. Talashilkar and O.P. Vimal, "From Nutrient-Poor Compost to High Grade Fertilizer," *BioCycle*, March 1984.

54. Martin Strauss, "About Wastewater and Excreta Use in India" (draft), World Health Organization International Reference Centre for Wastes Disposal, Duebendorf, Switzerland, June 1986.

55. See Richard G. Feacham et al., *Health Aspects of Excreta and Sullage Management—A State of the Art Review* (Washington, D.C.: World Bank, 1980); Shuval et al., *Wastewater Irrigation in Developing Countries*; Shuval et al., *Night-soil Composting*; and World Health Organization, *The Risk to Health of Microbes in Sewage Sludge Applied to Land* (Copenhagen: 1981).

56. Beltsville Aerated Rapid Composting System designed by USDA scientists, discussed in Shuval et al., *Night-soil Composting.*

57. Spirn, *The Granite Garden.*

58. Information on groundwater from Spirn, *The Granite Garden.*

59. Denver suburbs water purchases from Thomas J. Knudson, "Dry Cities of West Buy Up Farm Water Rights," *New York Times*, February 10, 1987; Catherine Caufield, "The California Approach to Plumbing," *New Scientist*, February 21, 1985.

60. Ian Douglas, *The Urban Environment* (Baltimore, Md.: Edward Arnold Publishers, 1983).

61. V. Nath, "Urbanisation in India: Review and Prospects," *Economic and Political Weekly*, Vol. 21, No. 8, February 22, 1986; water supply problems in Jakarta reported in Gunnar Lindh, *Water and the City* (Paris: United Nations Educational, Scientific and Cultural Organization, 1983); Manila sewage system information from DIESA, *Population Growth and Policies in Mega-Cities: Metro Manila.*

62. Fred Pearce, "Ring of water will end London's bursts," *New Scientist*, January 29, 1987.

63. Michael Browning, "For a town that's going dry, Peking treats water cheaply," *Miami Herald*, July 15, 1986.

64. Vinod Thomas, "Evaluating Pollution Control: The Case of São Paulo, Brazil," *Journal of Development Economics*, Vol. 19, 1985; figures on respiratory diseases in Calcutta from Hardoy and Satterthwaite, "Third World Cities and the Environment of Poverty."

65. Spirn, *The Granite Garden.*

66. Robert O. Boorstin, "Clean Air Deadline Nears, And City Ponders Its Choices," *New York Times*, October 26, 1986.

67. World Bank, *Urban Transport.*

68. Ibid.; and Steven R. Weisman, "What Works in Calcutta? A Subway," *New York Times*, March 21, 1987.

69. Kenneth D. Frederick, "Watering the Big Apple," *Resources* (Resources for the Future, Washington, D.C.), Winter 1986; Joyce Purnick, "Water Meters Due in All City Houses," *New York Times*, November 13, 1986.

70. Spirn, *The Granite Garden*; for further discussion of green belt and land preservation strategies, see Judith Kunofsky and Larry Orman, "Greenbelts and the Well-Planned City," *Sierra*, November/December 1985.

71. Rome's new auto restrictions reported in John Tagliabue, "Cars Face Rush Hour Ban in Central Rome," *New York Times*, February 22, 1987; automobile restrictions for other European cities from Spirn, *The Granite Garden*; for Hong Kong and Singapore, see World Bank, *Urban Transport*.

72. World Bank, *Urban Transport*.

73. Ibid.

74. Wendell Berry, private communication, April 15, 1987; see also Wendell Berry, *The Unsettling of America: Culture and Agriculture* (New York: Avon, 1977).

75. Scobie, "Food Consumption Policies."

76. DIESA, *Population Growth and Policies in Mega-Cities: Seoul*.

58

Lester R. Brown is President and Senior Researcher with Worldwatch Institute and Project Director of the Institute's annual *State of the World* reports. Formerly Administrator of the International Agricultural Development Service of the U.S. Department of Agriculture, he is author of several books including *World Without Borders, By Bread Alone, The Twenty-Ninth Day,* and *Building a Sustainable Society.*

Jodi L. Jacobson is a Researcher with Worldwatch Institute and coauthor of *State of the World 1987.* She is a graduate of the University of Wisconsin-Madison, where she studied economics and environmental sciences.

THE WORLDWATCH PAPER SERIES

Bulk Copies (any combination of titles)
2-5: $3.00 each   6-20: $2.00 each   21 or more: $1.00 each

Calendar Year Subscription (1987 subscription begins wth Paper 75)
U.S. $25.00 _____

Make check payable to Worldwatch Institute
1776 Massachusetts Avenue NW, Washington, D.C. 20036 USA

Enclosed is my check for U.S. $ _____

name _____

address _____

city   state   zip/country